D1576876

I2917274

The Same but Different

Molly Potter

ILLUSTRATED BY
Sarah Jennings

FEATHERSTONE
LONDON OXFORD NEW YORK NEW DELHI SYDNEY

This book is dedicated to Sue Garratt, my wonderfully astute friend who tells it like it is - with humour to boot!

FEATHERSTONE
Bloomsbury Publishing Plc
50 Bedford Square, London, WC1B 3DP, UK
29 Earlsfort Terrace, Dublin 2, Ireland
BLOOMSBURY, FEATHERSTONE and the Feather logo are trademarks of Bloomsbury Publishing Plc
First published in Great Britain, 2021 by Bloomsbury Publishing Plc
Text copyright © Molly Potter, 2021
Illustrations copyright © Sarah Jennings, 2021

A catalogue record for this book is available from the British Library

ISBN: HB: 978-1-4729-7802-8; ePDF: 978-1-4729-7798-4; ePub 978-1-4729-7799-1

2 4 6 8 10 9 7 5 3 1

Printed and bound in China by Leo Paper Products, Heshan, Guangdong

FSC
www.fsc.org
MIX
Paper from responsible sources
FSC® C020056

To find out more about our authors and books visit www.bloomsbury.com and sign up for our newsletters

Dear Reader,

The Same but Different is a book about how we can all be **different** from each other and also about how we can be the **same**. While it feels good to have things in common with other people, it's also really exciting to be different.

This book will help you understand that differences in others should be respected, celebrated and enjoyed. Difference makes the world a fun, exciting and interesting place. It really would be very boring if everyone was the same!

It's good to know...

Every one of us deserves to be respected and treated fairly. Sometimes people are unkind to those who are different from them. Anyone who does this needs to learn a better way to behave towards others.

Contents

We're all different

There are over seven billion people on Earth. Yet, even if you searched the world from end to end, you would never find two people exactly the same. Seven billion is a number far too big to imagine. It's easier to think about it this way: every minute about 250 babies are born. That is four babies born every second! And every single one of them is unique.

It's good to know...

Unique means being unlike anything or anyone else.

One billion looks like this in numbers: 1,000,000,000.

6

There's nobody exactly like you

There is not one single person on this planet who is exactly the same as you. It's also extremely unlikely that any two people would give identical answers to these questions. Try it on your friends and family and see!

Why not turn the page and explore this book to discover all the wonderful things that make us different.

We look different

You just need to look at another person to see all the ways in which you are different. This definitely makes the world a more interesting place. Imagine how confusing it would be if everyone looked exactly the same!

People can look different from each other because they...

Have different face shapes.

Have different skin colours.

Are different heights.

I grew a lot last night.

Have different eye colours.

Have different hair colours.

Have different hairstyles.

Wear different clothes.

Wear glasses (or not).

I love your glasses.

It's good to know...

Even identical twins that choose to dress the same can usually tell you about something that makes them look slightly different.

We can be good at different things

Nobody can be brilliant at everything. Sometimes we are naturally talented at something and find it easy to do, and other times we have to work hard at something to be good at it.

People can be good at different things, and this makes life interesting. For example, people can be good at...

Science.

Painting.

Giving compliments.

Making things.

It's good to know...

Trying hard to get good at something we find difficult takes loads of practice and a lot of bravery. Try to encourage your friends when they are finding something difficult – especially if it's something you find easy.

Playing music.

Being polite.

Why, thank you very much, this looks absolutely delicious. I appreciate the time you took to make this.

Exploring nature.

I love being outside.

Running really fast.

We like different things

We all like different things. Sometimes our friends really don't like something we love and sometimes they love something we hate. This is absolutely fine.

Here are some things people like and dislike. How do you feel about the following things?

Tomatoes.

Snow.

Getting up early.

Cooking.

We have different personalities

Personality is a word that describes how a person tends to think, feel and behave. We each have a unique personality. Your personality can be different from others in lots of ways but here are some examples. People can...

Be noisy or quiet.

Be messy or tidy.

You've got a bit of chocolate around your mouth.

Be funny or serious.

Prefer to have one or two good friends or have lots of different friends.

It's good to know...

Because everyone has different personalities, we appreciate or enjoy different things about our friends. You might like to be comforted when you are upset by one friend but enjoy how another friend makes you laugh.

We can have different opinions and beliefs

When you listen to what people are saying, sometimes you agree with them, sometimes you think differently and sometimes you learn something you've never thought of before.

People can have different opinions about...

Which season is best.

Which lesson at school is best.

Which animal they would like to be.

Their favourite painting.

People can have different beliefs...

About aliens.

Do you believe in aliens?

I think it's impossible to know if there are aliens out there.

About superstitions.

If you walk under that ladder, you'll have bad luck.

I don't believe that.

About whether ghosts exist.

I believe in ghosts.

I think ghosts are made up.

About God or gods.

I believe in God.

I believe in more than one god.

I don't believe in God.

It's good to know...

It's important to respect the opinions and beliefs of other people (as long as those opinions do not harm anyone).

Our families and homes can be different

We think about a family as two or more people who care about each other and who often spend lots of time together. People in families are related to each other in some way. Families can be different in lots of ways; here are just a few.

A family can...

Be really large (or really small).

Have two parents or one parent.

Include children who have been adopted.

Have step- or half-brothers or sisters who spend time in two different homes.

16

Our homes can...

Be different sizes.

Be different shapes.

I live in a flat on the 10th floor.

I live in a big house.

Be in different places.

I live in a city.

I live in the countryside.

Be really modern or really old.

It's good to know...

It doesn't really matter what type of home you live in. A home is about the people who live there and how much they care about each other.

We can speak different languages

There are over 7,000 different languages in the world and nobody could possibly learn them all. It's exciting to learn how to speak another language but it takes a lot of practice.

Some people speak one language.

I speak English and I'm looking forward to learning French when I'm older.

Some people can speak more than one language.

Jestem z Polski, ale potrafię też mówić po angielsku.

I'm from Poland but I can also speak English.

Some people move from one country to another and learn the language of their new country.

I'm from South Korea. English is my second language.

Some languages use a different alphabet, like Arabic and Japanese.

I love eating pizza.
أنا أحب أكل البيتزا.

Me too.
私も。

We can live in different places

People can...

Live in the same place all their life.

> I was born in London and have always lived here.

Move around and live in lots of different places.

> I'm a Traveller. I've called lots of places home.

Start life in one country, then move to another.

> I'm from Thailand. I moved to the UK when I was three.

Have parents who are from different countries.

> My mum is Norwegian and my dad is Indian. We all live in Britain.

It's good to know...

Some people live in the same place all their lives and others move away from where they were born. When people move to a new place we need to make them feel welcome.

We can celebrate different things

In most countries and religions, there are several celebrations that happen every year. Celebrations usually involve friends and family coming together, with decorations, special food and traditions. When people move to different countries they often bring their celebrations with them.

Here are just four examples of the many celebrations and festivals that happen each year.

Chinese New Year

Christmas

Diwali

Eid al-Fitr

We can do things differently

People from different countries do some everyday things in different ways.

Here are some examples.

In some countries like Japan it's considered rude not to slurp when eating noodles.

Can you do it for any less?

In some countries it's normal to haggle over the price of things.

In some countries like India people often eat food with their hands.

In many countries around the world, it's rude to point.

It's important to know...

The way we do ordinary things might seem strange to a person living somewhere else in the world.

Some differences you might have heard of

As we know, people can be different in lots of ways. Sometimes groups of people who share something in common have a word that describes their group. These words are only useful if a person wants to use them to describe themselves. Usually people just like to be called by their names.

Here are just a few of the words you might hear people use to describe themselves.

We can also be the same

Even though we are all different, you can usually find something that is the same or nearly the same about you and anyone you meet.

It's good to know...

It's always really nice when we find out we're the same as someone else in some way. However, it can also be exciting when we discover someone is different from us.

Humans are like one big family

Even though every person is unique, there are some things that are true about absolutely everyone in the world.

Everyone needs to eat.

Everyone feels uncomfortable when they get really hot or really cold.

Everyone began life as a baby who needed an adult to look after them.

Everyone has emotions.

Everyone in the world uses their brain to think and make decisions.

Everyone has an imagination.

Everyone feels pain.

Everyone likes to be liked, or better still, loved.

It's good to know...

In many ways, our similarities make us like one big family. While we are all individuals, we also share a lot of important things.

What do we all prefer ?

As humans, we all prefer...

Kindness to unkindness.

Smiles to scowls.

Compliments to insults.

I really enjoy playing with you.

Being helped rather than being ignored.

Being included rather than not being asked to join in.

To feel we belong rather than feeling like an outsider.

What do we all deserve?

Every single one of us deserves...

To be listened to, especially when we are unhappy about something.

To be given the same chances in a fair way.

To be treated with respect.

To be safe and not be harmed.

To be considered just as important as everyone else.

To have people who care about us – including friends.

Talking about diversity and differences with your child

There's no doubt that prejudice and discrimination, borne out of ignorance about diversity, can cause lots of unnecessary suffering and the world would be a much better place without either. If you're sharing this book with your child, then undoubtedly you want your child to grow up understanding diversity and celebrating difference. Here are some further tips to help you do this.

Acknowledge differences
This might sound obvious but to help your child embrace diversity, you need to acknowledge differences. Never avoid talking about a minority group because you're worried about getting questions you can't answer. Prejudice and discrimination can't be tackled head-on if groups that are the targets of these are not even acknowledged. However, it's also important for your child to know that most people prefer to be called simply by their name and not labelled with the name of a minority group they belong to.

Be a role model
Help your child to see that you truly celebrate diversity by being a role model. Demonstrate an inclusive attitude: by always valuing everyone's contribution, showing excitement about different cultures and respect for different beliefs, etc. A simple starting point for celebrating difference is helping your child understand that it's OK to hold different opinions. Find something you have a different opinion about, e.g. your favourite colour or lesson at school, and point out how it's interesting that you think differently. Chat about how boring it would be if everyone liked or did the same thing.

Expose your child to diversity
Encourage your child to watch TV programmes and films that include diverse characters and when possible, visit communities that have different cultures or beliefs from your own.

Choose books that reflect diversity
Select books by diverse authors and illustrators, that include diverse characters from different backgrounds and cultures, or that aim to educate children about lives different from their own.

Discuss stereotypes
If your child uses a stereotype, challenge it initially by asking them where they heard it. Help them understand how stereotypes can be harmful. The most obvious and easiest place to start is with gender stereotypes. Do all girls like pink? Do all boys love football? Talk about how these stereotypes can make you believe you should behave in certain ways. Discuss how a person might feel if they didn't obey these 'unwritten rules'. Explain that not everyone thinks of themselves as simply male or female.

Challenge prejudice

If your child makes a statement that is prejudiced, gently challenge it. Never overreact. The aim is to be careful not to make your child upset or defensive or they'll worry about asking questions. Let your child wonder about diversity. Children's questions can sometimes come across as inappropriate by an adult's standards, but are often asked out of genuine curiosity with no malicious intent. Respond to their questions, or explore the answers together so they learn to understand and celebrate diversity. Remember: stereotyping, prejudice and discrimination are learned and can therefore equally be unlearned.

Encourage empathy

Prejudice and discrimination stem from a lack of empathy. Encourage your child to put themselves in the shoes of someone who has experienced prejudice or discrimination to help them understand why it's wrong.

Consider identity and belonging

Help your child understand that as social animals, humans like to belong. We all belong to many groups, depending on our gender, neighbourhood, school, family, extended family, clubs, etc. This is fine as long as nobody feels excluded

because of who they are or what they believe. Anything that creates the idea of 'insiders' and 'outsiders' can build a sense of difference and create reasons to exclude people.

Finally... Educate yourself

If you've never had to think about difference and diversity, then you probably haven't experienced discrimination. It should never be assumed that tackling both prejudice and discrimination should be the responsibility of the minority groups who are being discriminated against. Educating yourself about issues specific to minority groups and becoming an ally means you not only demonstrate how to celebrate diversity to your child, but you also know how to challenge prejudice when you encounter it.

It's also important to remember that people don't necessarily want to be labelled by the minority group they belong to or constantly talk about their identity. There is plenty of material online that can inform you about diversity and inclusion. Also check if your local library runs a 'Human Library' as this can be a very quick way to become educated about a minority group.

Glossary

- **ADHD**
  a condition that affects people's behaviour. People with ADHD (attention deficit hyperactivity disorder) can seem restless and be impulsive

- **Adopted**
  when people legally take on the responsibility of bringing up a child that they were not the birth parents of

- **Autism**
  a condition that can be quite different in different people. It can mean the person with the condition does not find friendship skills straightforward, can have repetitive patterns of thought and behaviour and can struggle to change their routine

- **Belief**
  something that a person thinks is true, even if they can't prove it

- **Bisexual**
  someone who is attracted to more than one gender

- **Cisgenger**
  someone who identifies with and takes on the expression of the sex (male or female) they were assigned at birth. This is sometimes shortened to 'cis'

- **Disabled**
  when a person is physically disabled, they have a physical condition that can affect their movement, senses or how they carry out activities

- **Diwali**
  a five-day festival of lights celebrated by Hindus, Jains, Sikhs and some Buddhists

- **Eid al-Fitr**
  a religious holiday celebrated by Muslims. It happens at the end of Ramadan which is a month of fasting in daylight hours

- **Gay**
  a person who is attracted to members of the same gender

- **Immigrant**
  a person who has come to live in a country that they were not born in

- **Learning disability**
  having a learning disability means that people find it harder to learn certain life skills and might have difficulty with everyday activities

- **Mental illness**
  lots of different illnesses that can affect thinking, behaviour and mood

- **Mixed-race**
  people whose parents or ancestors are from different races or ethnic backgrounds (e.g. the child of one Black parent and one Asian parent would be mixed-race)

- **Opinion**
  what someone thinks about something. They are not the same as facts

- **Refugee**
  a person who was forced to leave the country where they lived because of war, persecution or violence

- **Transgender**
  anyone who expresses their gender differently to - or does not identify with - the sex they were assigned at birth. This is sometimes shortened to 'trans'